The Pain From Within

Overcoming Depression

Written By:
Easie Arceneaux

ISBN - 979-8-89660-440-2

Book cover design, editing format & layout: *Your Writing Table* (*www.yourwritingtable.com*)

CONTENT WARNING!

This book is for mature audiences as it contains potentially triggering & sensitive subject matter, including abuse towards children.
This book is not recommended for those under the age of 18.

Dedication

I truly dedicate this book to myself and everyone that's going through a tough time struggling with depression and anxiety. I can honestly say that writing this book has brought so much out of me that I never knew was hidden. I remember sitting in my closet in the dark really thinking about it all and how it started. That really brought me to tears and thinking about it still does, but I'm a survivor and I'm proud of how far I have come.

To my mom, kids, sisters and friends that were there for me also I'm truly honored for that. Depression is really real and I fight hard every day to stay focused. Yes, it's hard but I know God has a plan for me and I'm gonna keep holding on to His hand.

This book is in loving memory of both of my grandmother's Mary and Lavern who I miss so very much. Also, to my grandfather, Billy R McCray, who is truly missed.

The Pain From Within

To my best friend/cousin Gumarus S. Everett (Shumez), my aunt Carolyn Lewis Williams (Cat), Uncle Willis Lewis (Rock), and Patrick Wayne Lewis (Pat). You're not here on earth with me to witness the growth and my purpose of writing my book, but you're here in spirit with me at all times and I cherish that and always will until we meet again. I know you all are pushing and cheering me on in Heaven. I can't wait to see you again when it's my time. I love and miss you all dearly, especially my best friend Shumez. He always had a word for me and always kept it 💯 … I truly, truly miss him.

To my editor and writing coach: I trusted Ms. Chelsia's words of encouragement telling me that I got it. She never doubted me or my work and if I didn't know something she was only a phone call away and never said a mumbling word about negativity and I truly love her for that.

Table of Contents

The Pain From Within

Introduction

This book is based on true events that happened in my life and some of my loved ones connected to me.

Depression is something that I think everyone experiences at least once or twice in their life. It is definitely a pain that is within. Even as I was writing this book, I have seen the news reports of celebrities and other public figures that have committed suicide and family members or loved ones shared that the person did go through some depression. My heart goes out to them because I understand what they're going through. Depression can definitely turn into a silent killer if you don't get help.

It is possible to hide your depression and the people closest to you may not even realize what's going on. I was depressed for years; my husband and sister were also depressed, and people didn't know. I really believe my two boys were depressed, too, and didn't say anything or didn't know how to say it. We still went to work and lived our lives and went about our business but being broken and sad all the time. I could see my family being torn apart slowly.

The Pain From Within

The problem was that the depression was keeping me from living my life to the fullest. It was keeping my husband from being the best husband and father he could be. It was holding my sister down and not allowing her to live her life to the fullest. None of us really talked about it. It wasn't until I started writing this book that I was able to talk with my husband, sister, even my mother to find out how depression had affected each of them.

Everyone won't admit that they suffer from depression. Some people will tell you that they are going through it because they can see how you changed, but others may just hold it in and tell you they're okay when they really aren't.

Through this book, I pray I am able to share my story and my experiences and let you know that you *can* overcome depression. Even when you are at your lowest and saddest point, you can overcome and beat depression.

One of the most important things is to never give up on yourself. If you give up on yourself, you are not allowing anyone to help you and you are saying you don't want help... you want to stay depressed. So, I want to challenge you and encourage you to get help. Let your loved ones and professionals give you what you need to come out of the depression and start living your life. When you recognize the pain from within, you can start the journey to healing.

The Pain From Within

DEFINITIONS/COMMONLY USED WORDS

As we go throughout the book, there will be words used to describe some of the things I have experienced. Below are a few of the disorders and feelings that go along with depression.

Anxiety: Anxiety is an emotion characterized by feelings of tension, irritability, worried about many things on a daily basis, thoughts that keep you "on the edge," and physical changes such as increased blood pressure.

ADHD: Attention-deficit/hyperactivity disorder (ADHD) is a chronic condition that affects millions of children and often continues into adulthood. It can also include a combination of persistent problems, such as difficulty sustaining attention, hyperactivity & impulsive behavior.

Bipolar: Bipolar disorder is a brain disorder that causes changes in a person's mood, energy, and ability to function. People with bipolar disorder experience intense emotional states that typically occur during distinct periods of days to weeks, called mood episodes.

These mood episodes are categorized as manic/ hypomanic (abnormally happy or irritable mood) or depressive (sad mood). People with bipolar disorder generally have periods of neutral mood as well.

When treated consistently, people with bipolar disorder can lead full and productive lives.

Depression: Depression is a mood disorder that causes a persistent feeling of sadness and loss of interest and can interfere with your daily functioning.
***There is no cure for depression**. There is no cause for depression. It can occur for a variety of reasons, and it has many different triggers.

Psychotic Episodes (psychosis): Symptoms of psychosis include delusions (false beliefs) and hallucinations (seeing or hearing things that others do not see or hear). Other symptoms include incoherent or nonsense speech, and behavior that is inappropriate for the situation.

Trauma: A deeply disturbing and distressing experience or situation that happens to someone that can make you feel unsafe, scared and even paranoid that it could happen again. It can also be described as a type of emotional and psychological "shock" that happens after a very stressful, emotional, possibly violent situation that is difficult to cope/deal with. (Example: being in a car accident or seeing an accident happen in front of your eyes; death of a loved one; abusive relationships.)

STATISTICS/FACTS

- Nearly half of those with major depression also suffer from severe and persistent anxiety. People who are depressed often feel anxious and worried. One can easily trigger the other, with anxiety often preceding depression.
- There are 3 levels of depression: mild, moderate or severe; melancholic or psychotic.[1]
- People with low self-esteem who have a poor outlook or who feel overwhelmed by stress and feel that they aren't good enough.
- Depression is a brain disorder and a state of mind/how you think. It represents a very large portion of all mind-brain illnesses and it is connected to other mood disorders such as bipolar disorder, postpartum depression, PTSD (post-traumatic stress disorder, anxiety and suicide).

---

[1] Hope For Depression Research Foundation. (2022). Retrieved from: https://www.hopefordepression.org/depression-facts/?gclid=Cj0KCQiAqOucBhDrARIsAPCQL1asukiHlg2bdqbctAA8xiRd6ZcCO16yQuqn9MjTCU5y7u9LFADQO5MaAh58EALw_wcB

How depression feels

It's different for everyone. Below are some of the symptoms and common characteristics:

- Torture
- Feeling hopelessness
- Numbness
- Empty
- Feels like being run over by a big truck
- Feels like a heavy load on me at all times, sometimes too much
- Feels like nothing is ever going to be right
- It is always a fear of destroying everyone and everything I love
- Desperately wanting to be good enough for my kids and family I care about... Never feeling like I can live up to their expectations
- Feels like there's something missing and can't figure out what it is
- Existing but not living; drowning without a life jacket

**How does depression feel for you? What do you experience? List them below.
As you read through your list, begin thinking about how these things affect your everyday life...**

____

____

____

____

____

____

____

____

> ## You CAN overcome depression!

Recognizing the Signs:
When you know something isn't right

One of the first things that you need to pay attention to when it comes to depression is recognizing that something is not right with your feelings and your behavior. One of the most common symptoms of depression is constantly feeling down, sad, no energy, no excitement or desire to do anything, and you don't want to be around people. You don't want to be involved with normal, everyday activities. You prefer to be by yourself, separated from everyone else. And you may also think about your problems over and over again, all day and all night which cause you to feel even worse.

Another important thing that is really important to overcoming depression is recognizing and understanding how it started in the first place. What was the situation or event that happened? If you don't take the time to think about what happened to you that caused you to start feeling like this, it will be even more difficult for you to begin healing.

The Pain From Within

Depression is usually connected to something that happened in your life and it is usually a type of trauma. Maybe you had someone close to you pass away or maybe you broke up with your boyfriend or girlfriend. Or it could be that you lost your job or maybe your car was stolen. There are so many things that can cause you to become depressed.

There's a difference in depression and sadness, too. Sadness is not something that hangs around for weeks, months and years. Sadness comes and goes pretty quick. You can feel sad about something and it can usually by the next day or sometimes in a few hours, or until you aren't as sad anymore. Depression sticks around. Depression is like a bad cough that won't go away, and if you don't get help it gets worse and worse and some people actually commit suicide because the depression completely takes over their mind.

Yes, some people are sad all day. It's a constant, consistent feeling. Other people may have something happen to them that can cause the depression to appear. A few examples could be not getting enough sleep, you were a victim of a violent physical or sexual attack, they might be under a lot of stress at home or work (or both), there may be substance or alcohol use; or in women they may have some type of hormonal imbalance. This is part of recognizing and paying attention to what's going on in your life so you can get a better understanding of how and why you are depressed.

How do you know if you're experiencing depression? Here are a few signs:

- Feeling sad more than usual
- Losing interest in things you usually enjoy
- Change in your appetite (you're not as hungry as you used to be; no desire to eat)
- Problems sleeping
- No energy/feeling tired more than usual
- Feeling worthless
- Thinking about death or suicide

Depending on what happened and how serious it was can affect how you react to it. For example, if one of your parents passed away you will definitely be sad because they are gone. That sadness will cause you to cry and maybe you want to be alone or not be bothered. That is also known as grief, which comes and goes. Today you're sad but tomorrow or next week you aren't as sad; you feel better. Your self-esteem or your self-worth is not affected by their death.

Depression, on the other hand, means you are more than just sad. You have actually lost interest in living your normal, everyday life for more than just a few days. You feel worthless and like life doesn't matter now that this person you loved is not here anymore. When this happens, that situation or life event is called a **TRIGGER**.

Triggers are those things, people, situations that cause you to feel deep sadness, anxiety and stress. It can also be the anniversary date of a situation/event that happened to you. For example, some people become very depressed every year when September 11 approaches. This was when the planes hit the Twin Towers in 2001 in New York killing hundreds of people and the news channels showed it over and over for hours. Some people actually lost loved ones in that attack and those that watched it on TV were affected by the visual images. Those images can be triggers that cause you to be extremely sad and lead to depression.

There are times when friends and family can be the cause of these triggers. It's important to pay attention to conversations you have with certain people to protect your emotions at all times.

If you are talking with someone and you begin to see that every time you talk with them, you feel more angry than usual or you feel more upset and frustrated, it could be that that particular person may bring those emotions out of you. It may be in your best interest to not be around that person as much as possible. Protecting your peace is the most important thing.

Some of my greatest triggers have been people that were close to me. It took me a while to understand how and why they affected me like that but once I understood it, it helped me to set boundaries for myself. I also learned that some people can't be in my life anymore even if we were close at one time.

As you read the stories, think about these things:
- Do you have people in your life that are triggers?
- Do they cause you to feel a certain type of way which makes you feel depressed?

If you can answer yes to these questions, let's talk about it at the end of this section.

The Pain From Within

Trigger caused by a friend:

When I stated there is no cause or timeline for depression, that's exactly what I meant. It hits anytime – day or night – you can't control it. I have tried so hard to try and control it, but I couldn't take medicine every day. It made me sleepy and really made me feel worse sometimes. I couldn't stay closed up in my room all day, either because I had a family to take care of. It wasn't easy thinking that your family and close friends don't have your back because they don't understand what causes your depression. They look at you like you're going crazy and instead of trying to help, sometimes they make it worse, too.

When I was growing up, I had two best friends. One got into some trouble and went to prison for 15 years for not wanting to snitch, and my other best friend was out in the free world. We used to keep in touch all of the time until she met this guy. He was a real cool dude but when she began dating him, she slowly stopped contacting me, stopped coming by and that hurt me because she was the only friend I had at the time.

I became depressed and felt that way for a long time. I thought friends were forever; like sisters. I tried to figure out why she stopped contacting me but I didn't understand. I wasn't the type to go out or hang out a lot, and that may have been the reason but nothing made sense. Never in a million years would I think she would be that way with me.

Well, I was wrong. I was depressed and never told anyone what was wrong or how I was feeling. I put the situation in God's hands because if I was going to worry, I wasn't going to pray; but if I was going to pray, I had no reason to worry. So, I prayed and just left it alone.

After a while, God put it on my heart to contact her. I texted her brother and he gave me her new number. I texted her and shared what was on my heart.

She texted back: **Who is this?**
Me: **Your best friend.**
Her: **I don't have a best friend.**
Me: **Really?**
Her: **Yes, I don't have a best friend.**

Instantly, everything in me shut down because I felt she was like a sister to me. That's what I thought about our friendship. I cried and started thinking a lot of negative things that caused me to be even more depressed. I wondered how she could throw away a friendship from childhood.

I have not tried to contact her anymore since then because I felt she wasn't really a true friend if it was that easy to throw away a friendship. I accepted that our friendship must not have meant anything to her, and she didn't care about anything except putting out an image of someone she really wasn't.

My closure was putting her in my past, and she remained there until November 2022. God placed us at the same place at the same time because both of our kids had appointments at the same doctor's office. My friend noticed my son and then noticed me, and we started talking. I told her how I felt and she did the same. We exchanged numbers and maybe texted once or twice since then and that was it. I felt some relief in talking to her because we both said what we needed to say, and we agreed on going out to eat and talk. However, she never called and we never went to eat so I never got any final closure on our friendship.

Even though I never heard from her again, I made peace with the situation after the texts stopped. It was really okay with me, too, because I realized I can't change her and make her be my friend.

I would love to encourage anyone that if you have a best friend/sister and they're down with you like "four flats on a black-top" cherish them. Real friendships are something to hold on to.

LET'S TALK ABOUT IT...

Have you experienced anything like this with a friend or someone you thought was a friend?

____

____

____

____

How did you handle the end of your friendship? Were you able to receive closure?

____

____

____

____

Have you been able to move on and begin new friendships?

____

____

____

____

Family can also be some of the most significant triggers that can affect you the most. I believe it's because they are closer to you than friends or co-workers and your emotions are more connected.

I have experienced this for myself. I have gotten into disagreements with my family and they spread lies about me in public or on social media. This caused me to become depressed and I actually became suicidal. I felt like I was cornered or something. I felt that the things they were saying about me would cause people who didn't know me to think what they were saying was true. I literally had to keep paperwork and documentation on me to prove my innocence.

I made appointments to see my doctor so I could talk about what was going on and have a good cry with no one judging me. I was really difficult to talk or interact with my kids, because I didn't know how to put my feelings into words; or there were times when I just didn't feel like talking, so I would text them.

I hated being me at times because my family put this image out there to make it look like I was something that I wasn't. I didn't want strangers to think what they were saying about me was true. Because of this, I hid the pain and held it inside which wasn't good. Not being able to express myself or release the pain and my feelings only caused more anxiety and frustration.

My Dad

When growing up as a little girl in a house that had less love and more violence it was very traumatizing, and there were many times I didn't know if that day was gonna be a good one or a bad one. Don't get me wrong – there were "some" good days, but the bad days got to be too much. It got to the point my mom made the decision to leave Louisiana and come to Houston where her sister lived.

Mom waited until Dad was gone to work, then she packed a basket of clothes for all six of her kids. My oldest sister was about 12 at the time and she helped my mom with our trip to Houston.

It was a relief for all of us to leave because we didn't have to watch my mom get hit on and we would be able to live peacefully. I love my dad, yes I do, but he wasn't ready to be a father and didn't know how to treat a lady.

While growing up and trying to become a young

woman, I talked with my dad after moving to Houston, but there were times when I would forget he was available for me to talk to because my life was so messed up.

I had anger problems, I was depressed and always getting into fights. I didn't know why but I think it was because of what I saw as a young girl growing up without my dad. I will say my stepfather was in the picture since I was about 5 years old and he is still to this day and I'm 40.

We struggled when we moved to Houston. My mom was making about $2-3 per hour trying to support six kids. We were really grateful for my auntie who helped us out, along with my mom's cousins and a few friends. As we got older my dad helped a little, but not much. Then he felt we didn't need him which wasn't true. I thought that when you have daughters you would want to be there for them at all times to teach them how they should be treated when becoming young women, but that didn't happen.

I had anger problems, I was depressed and always fighting, not knowing why, but I think it was because of what I saw as a young girl and growing up without my father. I will say that my stepfather was in the picture since I was about 5 years old and he was there for me and my siblings.

The Pain From Within

I started growing closer to my biological father a couple years ago, around 2020/2021 but not how a father and daughter were supposed to be. I really enjoyed getting to know him. Things were going well until one day he started talking about some things he used to do when he was younger. His voice changed and he became an angry madman. Everything he was saying was negative and he said he meant every word.

It caused me to have a flashback when my two sisters and I were talking to my dad and he told us about the time when he and my mom were younger, and my mom would hang out with his cousin and talk to other guys. I asked him, "Really? Do you actually think Mom would cheat on you in front of your cousin?"

He said, "Yes, she did that." I couldn't believe it. Wow! His cousin and my mom were best friends and hung out all the time. I asked why would she let my mom talk to other men knowing how my dad was and what he was capable of doing to her if he found out? Just hearing him say things like that, then thinking it's cool to say it made me really angry. I know I was young and I couldn't help her but I became depressed and that became a trigger for me.

After some years passed and I was a teenager, I would stay with my sister for a while or even go to my grandmother's house. We still had little to do with my dad because of all the damage he had done to my mom and to us.

He did nothing to help with expenses for me or my siblings when it came to making sure we had clothes, toiletries or even food. To see other friends with both their parents or even single moms taking care of their kids kinda bothered me because most of them had a dad who contributed to their well-being. It made me wonder why my dad didn't care to do the same thing for us.

There was a period of years that was silent before I was able to have a conversation with him. I had great depression knowing he was able to help but did nothing. I began to spiral negatively and I would act out in school, or whenever a situation or problem came up, I made it escalate.

I wanted to break the cycle and my dad knew what he had done to us was toxic. I was able to pull myself up, realized it was my depression that caused me to have these feelings. I knew I had to get a hold of it, especially because I had my own kids and I had to break the cycle. My relationship with my dad is now in a great place. We talk almost daily and he calls regularly to check on everyone.

<u>My Mother</u>

When it comes to depression, my mom says during the time she and my dad were together, going to church was always her comforter. When enough was enough, she decided to leave. She had a sister in Houston and planned to go there with her kids.

On the highway out of Louisiana, she could finally breathe. Raising her kids was second nature. She got a job immediately and lived with sister for a few months and then got a place of her own. Once again tried to make it work with our dad but immediately saw the same characteristics as before and knew immediately she had outgrown that chapter of her life.

She found a lady at work who immediately became her best friend, her counselor and confidante. She helped her navigate throughout that period, and to this day they are still the best of friends. Now she enjoys her entire life with God being the center of her life. It took years for my mom to even hold a conversation with my dad and now he has the utmost respect for her and will be there for her if she chooses to.

My Husband *(in his own words)*

Being diagnosed with depression causes a persistent feeling of sadness and loss of interest.

I was around 12 years old when I realized I was always in a bad mood, acting out and would lose interest in things quickly. Around 2006, my depression got worse and I was on the verge of losing my family. My wife told me to go get some medical help or she was leaving. During that time, I found out I was bipolar. I was prescribed medication and assigned a counselor. That worked well for a couple of weeks until I lost interest and stopped taking my medication.

Around 2016, my depression got so bad I decided to take my life by taking a bottle of pills. My mom found me passed out on the bathroom floor. I was rushed to the hospital where they had to pump my stomach, then they sent me to a psych hospital where they diagnosed me with depression and bipolar. I was able to overcome that experience by taking my medication as prescribed, meditation and prayer. If I was to help others, I would tell them to please take their medications as prescribed.

Around that time, I had stress coming from different angles. I just came home from prison for the second time and was trying to stay on the straight path. I was on parole again, dealing with the system. If you've been on probation or parole before, you know how stressful it can be especially when you're living in the same environment you went to prison from.

My wife and I were arguing so much to the point where we split up. I'm not gonna lie, just coming home from doing two years to being with my family only to separate from them again took a toll on me mentally. A big mistake I made and truly regret was not taking prescribed medicine to treat my depression. Instead, I treated it with a drug known as PCP. A couple of months later at my breaking point, I broke and it almost cost me my life.

That was six years ago and I still have my days; some more stressful than others. I no longer have the urge to commit suicide again and my purpose has been to leave as many memories with my kids before I do leave this Earth. That has been my medication nowadays, and it's actually working. I don't get in trouble with the law anymore.

My wife and I are back together; yes, like any other couple we have our moments but those are rare now. I no longer use PCP anymore and I just take it day by day, change the things I can pray to Allah to help me on the things I cannot. I can also focus on my kids and their happiness calms my depression.

LET'S TALK ABOUT IT...

As you read these stories, how did they make you feel?

____

____

____

Were you able to relate to any of the situations?

____

____

If yes, how did you handle being around those particular family/friends?

____

____

____

____

Did you find yourself turning to drugs or alcohol or other things to cope/make it through the day?

____

____

____

It's a Silent Destroyer...

This is the part that doesn't get talked about as much as it should. Depression is something that can tear families apart and cause many, many problems. Marriages can end, parents and children can stop talking, sista-girls and guys and their buddies can stop hangin out with each other.

We talked about the fact that people who suffer from depression can begin using drugs or alcohol just to try and deal with their feelings or remain isolated and by themselves because they don't want to be bothered. One of the symptoms of depression is staying to yourself. There's just something about being alone that makes you feel better, but you also don't like it at the same time. Sometimes you want to be around people and sometimes you don't. There were lots of times I preferred to be by myself because I didn't want to talk about how I felt or try to make people understand me.

Below are a few more stories about myself and my children. You will be able to see for yourself what happened and how it affected our family as a whole. I pray you are encouraged and find hope in the things we experienced.

My story *(in my own words)*

I have been diagnosed with manic depression. When I'm having an episode I don't feel comfortable being around anyone because I have all kinds of thoughts racing in my head. I stay shut up in my room which is dark; no light at all. I feel real hopeless, no energy suicidal thoughts. I feel that I carry a lot so I keep myself busy to not feel the way I do because if not I will shut down. I also suffer from anxiety and that's my worst feeling because I feel as if I can't concentrate and very nervous with my heart just racing.

I often sit and wonder, *Why me? Why me?* I need to know… I wanna know… I constantly think about it. My depression is hard to deal with because it's never a dull moment for me. My mind is constantly going and thinking about stuff that makes me feel worse and worse.

I lost four loved ones who I was really close to and cherished. My grandmother, L.V. Lewis passed August 23, 2009, which was way too early. I wasn't ready. My aunt, Caroly Lewis Williams passed Jan 16, 2020, which was also too early.

And what took the cake was when I got a call that my cousin, Gamarus Everett, who was serving a life sentence in prison got killed. That really hurt my heart because my cousin was my best friend. He was my go-to person whenever I was down and when he had problems, he called me and we wrote letters. He had been locked up since 1999, and he told me he would like to see the world through my eyes.

I miss him dearly; he was really my best friend when I had no one to talk. He was there for me. No one felt the pain like I felt. I still have the letters we sent to each other. My pain doesn't get better because I'm still grieving my grandmothers, L.V. and Mary McCray, too. I still look at her picture when she took her last breath laying in her bed at home and I cry just about all the time. I miss her so much.

When dealing with depression, it's hard to battle death alone. You can say you're fine but in reality you aren't, especially when you were close with that person. It's not easy to adjust to the fact that you won't be able to talk to them or see them anymore.

I always wonder how did I get here to this point? I never had the perfect moment with anything or anyone at all. I've always struggled mentally, physically and emotionally with everything and everyone! Not knowing why or what's going on with me. I've always been the one to help everyone but no one never helped me when I needed it. My mom, daughter and sister helped me during my battles with depression and anxiety really bad, but they're able to help me and be there for me when I'm struggling more than usual.

I'm so, so grateful every day that the Lord wakes me up and keep his arms around me. My daily struggle is to keep my sanity because mentally my mind is not right. Physically, I'm tired of the abuse and emotionally I'm tired of feeling angry or afraid of what might happen.

As I sit and think about all that I'm going through as an adult, I saw so much growing up. I saw the hurt and abuse that my mom went through. Sometimes I ask myself if what I'm going through now is what I saw in my past? Yes, it is! I saw my mom being beaten all the time and there was nothing I can do. I would see my sister and other family trying to help fight him (my dad) off of her. I was helpless to my mom!! But when we got away from him and left Louisiana we were fine with my auntie and her son. Unfortunately, when I got older I was a terrible little girl and I stayed in trouble. I was always doing something I shouldn't have, but I think I was acting out from everything that I had experienced.

In 1995 I think I was around 12 or so, and I was always in trouble getting kicked out of school and things like that. I just didn't know why I acted so horrible. In school I was fighting the teacher and students, throwing tables and chairs, kicking doors and cursing the grownups out like they were nothing and never wonder why all that was happening to me. I guess from seeing it when I was little it just caught up with me. I was always depressed and having thoughts of harming myself. Lord why?

How did I get here? So many times my thoughts drift and I wonder when did the depression and anxiety actually start? Was it when I was an adolescent and didn't know it? In April 1994, I was really out of control. I was so bad at school I got kicked out for fighting.

The Pain From Within

In October 1996, I was 13 years old and I used to always say "I wish I was dead" or "I wanna die." I never knew how I would I do it or anything. I just kept thinking I would be better off dead than alive, and out of everyone's life. Well, that didn't happen because my mom took me to see a psychiatrist and I had to go to a behavior group meeting every Wednesday. I thought that was helping but it really wasn't and I wondered why but never could get an answer.

My thoughts and behavior got worse to the point I was hearing voices talking to me and telling me bad things. My mom ended up admitting me to Chimney Rock Center. I asked myself why did she do that to me? My dreams and thoughts got worse to where I had to sleep in the room by myself and I started seeing the devil (fireman).

At first, I had a roommate because it was two beds in each room. The devil was right in front of me tempting me to kill myself. I was crying in my sleep because I was so scared. My roommate shook me until I woke up and I snapped out of the nightmare.

The next day they called my mom to pick me up because they were discharging me. They said I had to leave the facility because they couldn't handle suicidal thoughts. Looking back, I was really going through it and didn't realize it. Now that I'm older, I still deal with those same thoughts and that worries me. Depression is really real. Never let anyone tell you different. It is seriously a silent killer.

It wasn't until recently that now I know my dad is part of the cause of me feeling this way. I needed my dad then and still do to build a better relationship. My stepdad is who taught me and my siblings about life growing up. He made sure we were ready for whatever came our way. Do you know you can love someone dearly but in reality you hate them? I don't want to hate anyone because I can't make it into heaven with hatred in my heart. So, I have to forgive in order to move on with my life if my dad is in it or not; I'm grown now.

My stepdad always tells me to forgive those that have wronged me or took advantage of me, used me and always looked down on me. I've learned that maybe if I set things right in my life my depression may ease up and not be as intense. I know it's not gonna totally go away but there are better days ahead.

My baby boy

He suffers from ADHD and Bipolar Disorder. When my son has an episode he shuts down not saying a word to anyone.

He tells me how he acts like everything is cool when the truth is that everything is *not* cool with him. He tells me to be real I don't wanna be here on earth no-more!! I ask him why he would say that? He says he is a really big disappointment to everyone. I tell him all the time that he is never a failure to me or anyone else regardless I'm always going to help him whenever he has an episode.

I always keep an eye on my baby boy because I never know what crosses his mind because he would leave and text me when he gone live your best life and that's scares me a lot with him because he sits quiet like nothing bothers him and he holds everything in. I monitor my kids at all times because I know that mental illness can take you out when you least expect it.

When he was about 4 years old I took him and my other two kids to an appointment, which was a disaster, but when we left Addrick (my baby boy) had covered my eyes while driving. He had covered them so tight that I couldn't see so I had to let my daughter (who was 11yrs old at the time) drive us home because he told me his daddy said to kill me which was not true.

On February 6, 2023, I admitted my son into a

psychiatric hospital because he wanted to commit suicide. He was hearing voices telling him to do bad things to people and some of the words would be scrambled and he couldn't understand. I begged and pleaded for him to just talk to me, but he was not trying to talk or trying to hear me at all.

He asked, "You're gonna take me to the hospital or not?"

I agreed, so I picked him up from school then took him. We were there for about an hour doing the assessment and talking to the doctor when he looked at me and asked if we could leave. I said, "No, we're here now and we can't leave because they locked the doors behind us. Plus, they have to get your paperwork together."

He stayed at the hospital for 8 days doing group meetings, talking to the therapists and psych doctors. They put my son on different meds and gave him a paper to look at for coping skills. He was discharged on Valentine's Day, Feb 14,2023, and he went back to school the next day. He thought he was okay and we felt like everything was back to normal.

Before school was over, my son text me and asked me to pick him up. I asked him was he okay and he said no, he was still hearing voices!! I jumped up and picked him up from school with tears in my eyes. *Why was this still happening to him?* I asked myself.

I told him we needed to talk to his principal and he yelled, "NO!! I don't wanna go back to the hospital!"

I said, "No, you're not going back there. I'm gonna help you the best way I can." I told him that he gotta stay in church and hear the Word of God so that he would know how to fight back at Satan.

Going to church has really been helping him with his daily life until he went to school one morning. March 6,2023 he found out through one his friends that his homeboy had killed himself. He texted me and I was in shock. (This is the actual chat in his words.)

My son: "*My potna jus killed his self* 💔 💔 💔 😔 😔"!!
Me: *How? why? And who told you that?*
My son: *My potna jus told me it's going around now... Bro, he made sure he shake my hand everyday, Broooo like even if I didn't see him he saw me and came and shook my hand. This hurts for real !!!*
Me: *Damn.*
My son: *I'm crying real tears, bro. I had to come to the sac room.*

The SAC (Special Assignment Class) room is where they go for in-school suspension or if a student is having a hard time and needs to be separated from other students for awhile to get themselves together.

I had to go get him because he wanted to be alone... When I tell you from the time I picked my son up from school he cried and cried until he went to sleep and he still was in disbelief and was saying he should've known sooner that he was going through something.

I told him, "You see why I'm trying to keep you on your meds and in church because this shit is real for real. Depression is real."

Never give up on your kids when they need you the most because you never know what they're going through or trying to tell you. I pay close attention to my kids at all times and I make sure they're never alone because I'm here 100% of the way.

<u>My oldest son</u>

He suffers from ADHD, bipolar, schizophrenia and psychotic episodes. When he was about 6 years old I realized there was a change in my son's behavior, and at first I thought he was just being a kid. He wasn't just being a kid, though; he had a behavior problem that needed my attention more and I did just that gave him my undivided attention. Of course, I did everything that a parent would do and it still wasn't enough. I had tried different counseling services until I thought I found a male counselor.

We had sessions with him for about a week and it felt like we weren't getting anywhere because instead of him trying to find out about what's going on with my kids he wanted to know more of *my* personal life and about my kids' father. I got mad and said the hell with it because my son really needed help and I didn't need him digging all in me and my husband's business.

So, we were fortunate enough to meet this lovely lady near our home that started seeing my three kids. She was so lovable, caring and understanding; always helping me or trying to figure out ways to help me get the help I needed from other places.

On this one particular day I had taken him and my other two kids to an appointment (which turned out to be a mess). We went into her office and she said she had to meet with the kids separately. When I tell you my son got angry and started tearing up the place and talking bad to me and the lady.

Adrian would hear voices telling him to get into fights with people at school. My son used to run in the middle of the road for cars to hit him, he used to beat on people's cars, he used to break everything I had; he would beat his head on the walls/concrete or whatever, curse grownups out; he used to hear voices telling him to do bad things and still do. He would think people were talking about him when they're not.

I had taken him to the psych hospital plenty of times and he had to stay 7 days every time he went. I never had time to myself because he was my behavioral child and my sick child that needed me more not knowing I needed help myself with manic depression.

My depression was so bad that whenever we were in public he would clown me or throw food and other things down in the grocery store and run around screaming and hollering at me. I would stand there and cry feeling so embarrassed and ashamed in front of everyone and my daughter would tell me not to cry. I didn't know how to handle it. It was horrible but I am grateful to God that he has come a long way and changed. He still fights with the voices and have his bipolar moments but there not as bad as they used to be.

My oldest sister

I remember being about 5 years old, always sitting in the living room getting ready for church on Sunday morning. After my aunt or uncle dressed me for church, they sat me in front of the television to watch wrestling.

I can't quite remember on what days, but my aunt worked at a clothing or thrift store and while she was gone, she left me with her husband at the time. I didn't know what was going on when she would leave home. At that time, we lived in a 3-bedroom brick house, dining area to the left of the house, and the living room was when you came through the front door of the house. The television was to the right of the front door and the kitchen was to the left if you walked through the living room. The first room was to the left then it was another room to the left and the bathroom in the middle of those rooms, then another bedroom to the right.

My uncle lived down the street, I believe. I think he

may have been working at the time but he lived on the same street as my aunt and grandparents. My aunt had one son and I lived with them. Her son, my cousin, would have family and friends come over and they would hang out in the yard.

My aunt always took people in, but this one particular aunt, well, it was my aunt's sister-in-law, would always come over while my aunt was at work. Her and my uncle would go in the bedroom and make all of us kids go outside. My cousins had to go outside, but I guess because I was still little, they let me stay inside but I was told to stay in the living room and watch TV. My uncle's wife and my aunt's "husband" would be in the first bedroom to the left side of the house while I was in the living room sitting on the floor.

Also, during the times when my aunt was at work and if my "uncle" was not working, he started making my cousin and all the boys to stay outside. He would go into the same bedroom on the left side of the house and sit on the edge of the bed, which was kind of high. He would pull his pants down and sit on the edge of the bed, then tell me to come in the room.

The Pain From Within

When I got in there, he would ask me if I wanted my ice cream and to come on. I didn't know any better, so I walked over to him and he would pull his penis out and I had to perform oral sex on him. He would say, "Good girl," then I would go back in the living room and watch TV or whatever. He would tell me to sit down like nothing happened.

One day, my aunt's sister-in-law came over and while all the boys were outside including her own son and my aunt's son, I was the only one in the house. I walked in that first bedroom to the left and my uncle and aunt's sister-in-law was having sex. Mind you, she came over all the time while my aunt was at work. On this day, I called my aunt and told her what I saw. She came home and saw for herself, too. That was the reason they told the kids to stay outside and I was in the living room.

I had never told anyone before that day until I was 32. I told my daughter because I was embarrassed and ashamed of the situation and what people might say. I felt worthless and I thought I was going to lose my aunt. She was the one I felt had always been there for me through thick and thin out of all my family. I didn't want to lose her because she never knew what happened with her husband and what he made me do.

I know we aren't supposed to hate, but to this day, when I look at men it makes it hard for me to love. I know all men are not alike but because of my depression and anxiety, it makes it hard. Going through things like drinking and using drugs and being put in a mental hospital has brought me a long way. I do think about all of the things that happened to me on a day to day basis, but I have never been to a drug rehab facility.

With the help of the staff and therapists at LBJ Mental Health hospital in Houston and Ben Taub Neuropsychiatric department, I have been taught how to forgive. I can't forget the person that did those things to me, but I know only God can take care of him. I hope and pray every day that whatever woman this animal has come in contact with that they don't stay silent as long as I did and have the strength to come forth. I pray she won't feel ashamed or afraid of what someone may say or how they feel towards them when they choose to share that experience.

I remember when my aunt's brother would get me dressed on Sundays and sit me in front of the TV with popcorn to watch wrestling. Since I was holding all of this in, my way of dealing with it when we moved to Texas, I lived with my aunt in the Northpoint Apartments in the Greenspoint area.

I would be afraid to sleep by myself so my aunt's son (my cousin) would sit beside the bed and sing me to sleep. That's how I learned the song "As We Lay" by Shirley Murdock. As time went on and I got older, it bothered me more and more when I laid down at night. What people didn't know is that I would cry myself to sleep and I couldn't seem to get over it.

In 2009, I lived in the Oak Ridge Apartments and worked at the Woodwind Lakes nursing home when I had a bad breakdown then ended up in a mental hospital. When I was released, I wasn't taking my medication like I was supposed to and I stayed depressed. I began smoking crack to keep my mind at ease and off of the things I didn't want to think about. I kept on using until I decided to get admitted again into the mental institution. When I was released that time, I promised myself I would leave the drugs alone, but depression kicked in again and I began using that same day.

The very next day, though, I said, "I quit" and I knew I had to get my life together. Ever since January 22, 2021 I have not used anymore and I have not looked back. (I have been sober and clean for two years now!! I know it was nobody but God!)

That time in my life had me so messed up that I hated men. I would see men and every single man was no good, a pervert, or whatever it was for me to see "bad" in a man. I had to tell myself, no more drugs and all men are not alike. I know that I suffer from being alone and even though I want to live alone, to this day I am still trying to work through those feelings.

I want to live by myself once my son goes to college, but my anxiety is really bad and I can't stand to be in crowds or large, noisy groups. I don't like people talking at the same time and I don't like a lot of company. I will have some company so I won't be alone and I'm trying to get away from feeling like that. I still suffer from depression, so I try not to think about things that my family or my kids go through because I bring their issues on myself and I get even more depressed thinking about them.

The way I deal with depression now is to take my

medication, think positive thoughts, keep working, keep negative energy and people away from me, and I find more positive things to do with my time. I exercise, watch TV and I have a new male friend I have been seeing for about 8 months. Since my last relationship (ordeal), he has been my shoulder to cry on and a friend to help me walk through being happy and not broken

Defeating Depression!

Depression is not something that has to take over your life forever. You CAN overcome depression and regain your life!

One way to do this is to focus on God's Word. Reading and meditating on the scriptures will help you to stay encouraged and remind you of God's promises for your life. When we allow God to be part of our healing process, things can turn around faster than we expect! I know this to be true.

Below are some of my favorite scriptures... what are yours? Write them down and use them as a reminder when times get hard.

Bible Scriptures

Philippians 4:6-8
Isaiah 41:10
Psalms 118:6
Joshua 1:9
Psalms 34:17-18
Mark 3:1-20

What are some of your favorite scriptures?

The Pain From Within

Use the box below to write as many as you like.

Easie Arceneaux

Music is another way that I am able to stay connected to God and keeping myself positive and encouraged. Sometimes music can talk to you in ways that can lift you up and make you feel so much better!

Below are some of my favorite songs. List yours below, too! Let the rhythm take you to a positive place!

"Bow Down & Worship" – Bishop Paul S. Morton
"Better Day" – Le'Andria Johnson & Donald Lawrence
"You Don't Know" – Donald Lawrence & Zacardi Cortez (my #1 favorite!)
"Grateful" – Hezekiah Walker, Dave Hollister & LFC

What are your favorite songs? Use the box below to write as many as you like.

> **You can say you're fine,
> but you really aren't...**

Speak Life, Not Death

Saying positive things is one of the best ways to change negative thoughts and begin to shift your mindset.

On the previous page, I shared some of my favorite scriptures. You can read those scriptures, then say it out loud to remind yourself of God's Word and to help you feel better and become stronger.

Joyce Meyer wrote a book that is so powerful when it comes to changing your thoughts. It's called "Battlefield of the Mind" and she talks about how we can renew and actually turn negative thoughts into positive ones. She uses scriptures to help you recognize negative thoughts and how to overcome them.

The Word of God says in 2 Corinthians 10: 3-5 that the weapons of our warfare are not flesh and blood, humans… they are all spiritual. We can't win the battle in our minds with guns and knives like we would a fight. The only way we can overcome things like depression is by actually changing our *mind*. It's a mind thing and it's not easy to change our minds. I guess that's why Mrs. Joyce calls her book "Battlefield" of the Mind because we are in a battle with our own minds.

Another scripture says the power of life and death is in our tongue. (Proverbs 18:21) We have the power to say positive things or negative things… build ourselves up or tear ourselves down. We have the choice.

I had to learn how to say positive things to build myself up when I was down. My daughter would remind me of how much she loved me and appreciated me for the sacrifices I made being a mom for her and her brothers. It's easy to forget when you have done good things or you know you're a good person when depression kicks in. Speaking positive things over myself made a huge difference in my life.

Say this out loud: **I have the power to speak LIFE over myself!**

Say it out loud at least 3 or 4 times until you feel it get down in your soul.

Say this one, too: **I CHOOSE to say positive things!**

Go back to your favorite scriptures and repeat the whole thing or whatever sticks out the most to you. I'll do mine that I shared with you in the previous section.

Philippians 4:6-8 – **I do NOT have to be anxious about anything! God's peace protects my heart & my mind!**

Isaiah 41:10 – **I do NOT have to be afraid! God will strengthen me & help me!**

Psalms 118:6 – **The Lord is on my side. I will NOT be afraid!**

Joshua 1:9 – **God has commanded me to be strong & courageous! I don't have to be afraid because God is with me wherever I go!**

Psalms 34:17-18 – **When I cry out for help, God hears me! He rescues me from ALL my troubles.**

The Pain From Within

Here are more affirmations you can speak out loud to help fight off negative thoughts when they enter your mind:

- I am learning to love myself more & more each day
- I am worthy
- I see the good in me
- I am growing everyday
- I will not let the past define me
- It's OKAY to not be perfect
- I will never give up on myself
- I CAN get through this
- I WILL get through this
- Depression is strong but with God, I am STRONGER!
- I have hope in tomorrow
- Depression will NOT break me
- I have the strength I need to get through this
- I believe & I know the best is yet to come
- What I see on social media does not define me
- What God has for me is for me
- I will give myself grace
- Sadness and depression does NOT define me
- I will not focus on the "what if's" that may not even happen
- I will not allow negative thoughts to overtake me
- This darkness will not last forever

- I CHOOSE to focus on positive thoughts & good things
- I am surrounded by people who love me & want me around
- I am able to find joy in everyday moments
- I am a work in progress & I welcome new beginnings
- I remind myself that each day is a gift and I am blessed to see each day and experience new things

It's your turn!

Write your own affirmations that you can say over & over again. You can even put them on sticky notes or tape them to your mirror so you can see them every day as reminders!

____

____

____

____

____

____

____

____

____

____

____

Below are some things you can say and do for those who are experiencing depression. You may not have the solution for their problem, but if they know you are supporting them and you love them, it can make a big, big difference!

ENCOURAGING WORDS/REMINDERS

- You're not alone
- I'm here for you no matter what
- It's okay to not be/feel okay
- You are not a failure
- Your story isn't over (if your loved one is having suicidal thoughts, they may feel like there's no point to living or their life is already over)
- Be good to yourself
- This is what you're going through, not who you are
- I hope you are surrounded by people who are good for your spirit
- You are amazing for facing this with so much courage and hope

OTHER WAYS YOU CAN HELP

- Staying in touch with loved ones by messaging, texting, calling or meet up for coffee, lunch, etc.
- Accepting them for who they are without judging them

- Try to be patient with them if they appear irritated or agitated
- Be understanding if they are slow to want to hang out or do things with family/friends

SELF CARE

- Challenge negative thoughts
- Get enough sleep
- Do something new
- Eat healthy
- Take deep breaths
- Take time for YOU and be unapologetic about caring for yourself
- Count to 10 slowly

SET BOUNDARIES

- Don't take things personally
- It is okay to say NO
- Take a firm stand against abusive/toxic behavior
- Do things you enjoy & love
- Do not enable your partner/children/friends
- Keep conversations & interactions short with people who you know can be a trigger for your emotions
- Block & delete numbers from your cell if it's not good for you to talk to certain people that can cause triggers
- Find closure & acceptance
- I have faith in God to help me heal, grow and get stronger each day

I Am An Overcomer!

I haven't overcome completely; I still suffer from depression, but it's not as bad as it used to be. I try not to dwell on my problems and it helps a lot when I'm with my doctor or my daughter. My doctor, daughter and my mom all listen to me when I'm having a breakdown and it helps when they show support and encourage me.

I have a positive mindset and outlook on life because I'm determined to stay focused on the good things that God has in store for me. I always make God my #1 priority even when I'm feeling my worst. It's in those times I notice that He works miracles in my favor!

With my mental illness, I try my best to keep live life as normally as possible but emotions can get me all messed up with no warning or anything. I don't know what to expect sometimes because I can be riding in the car, a song will come on the radio that will remind me of everything I've been through and then I want to shut down or I will shut down.

The Pain From Within

Having a support team is one of the best things you can have when fighting depression. My mom would always remind me of God's Word and she would give me scriptures like 2 Corinthians 1:3-4 that says: *"Praise be to the God and Father of our Lord Jesus Christ, the Father of compassion and the God of all comfort, who comforts us in all our troubles, so that we can comfort those in any trouble with the comfort we ourselves receive from God." (NIV)*

I also have an amazing true friend who helps me work through my moments when I am triggered; even when I feel ashamed and I know it's something I can't control. I'm just glad he is there with me, giving me encouraging words when I shut down and he helps me talk about what's going on when I can't get the words out correctly.

Depression takes a toll on me, especially when I have panic attacks and it causes me to breathe really heavy and my chest is tight. After an episode like that, I'm really tired and I just have to lay down and let it pass because there's nothing I can do about it. I do take my medicine and as I said before, I keep God first and those things do help.

At the time this book was written, I am happy to say my kids are doing great! My two boys have graduated from high school and they are both fathers with daughters. I still keep them encouraged and try to make sure I am fair with them and make sure they see things so they can make the best decisions for their lives. There is no perfect way to parent. All we can do is give our children the tools to help them in life and pray they use them wisely.

I didn't talk about her much, but I do have one daughter and she's 24 years old. When raising her, I had no problems. She is really my best friend and my comforter when I'm having bad days. She is a great listener and she also doesn't pick sides with her brothers or anyone else. She remains neutral and helps me keep the peace in the house.

When I have my breakdowns, she's the one I can count on to lift me up and make sure everything is good with me. I am truly grateful for her and I wouldn't trade her for anyone or anything.

Sadly, my husband and I are not together. We are separated and I try to stay cordial with him because of our kids. Marriage isn't guaranteed and I realized that we may not be right for each other. You have to love yourself as well as your partner and never allow yourself to be taken advantage of.

I close by leaving you with this – Living and loving yourself is the key because you can't be right for anyone else until you are right within him in order to truly value and love the "you" He created.

Notes...

Notes...

Notes...

Notes...

Notes...

**Depression did NOT
break me!**

About the Author

Easie Arceneaux is originally from Louisiana but moved to Houston, Texas at an early age and has been there ever since. She is married and has 3 children – 2 sons and 1 daughter.

In her free time, she enjoys relaxing at home and spending time with family. She also loves listening to music and dancing.

When she's not relaxing, she is trained and certified in braiding hair and installing weaves so she does hair "all the time!" In addition to doing hair, she also is a home health care provider.